Reaching the Summit

AVOIDING AND REVERSING DECLINE IN THE CHURCH

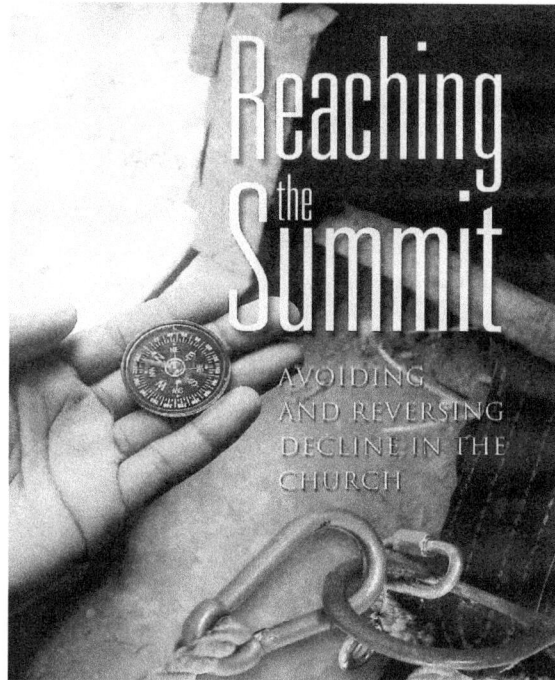

Study and Implementation Guide

Developed and written by:

George L. Yates

SonC.A.R.E. Ministries

SonC.A.R.E. Ministries

Christ's Awareness Raised Everyday

Website: soncare.net

Contents

The material in this publication is written with the intent to be studied alongside of REACHING THE SUMMIT: *Avoiding and Reversing Decline in the Church*. Participants will need access to a copy of the REACHING THE SUMMIT book to complete the content of this publication.

Avoiding and Reversing Decline in the Church Implementation Guide
Itroduction: Using This Material

The material in this workbook is intended to serve as a guide to be used alongside the book *Reaching the Summit: Avoiding and Reversing Decline in the Church*. The intent is to assist organizational leaders in searching with an open heart the needs of the organization. Then developing and implementing strategies and practices to build a sustainable healthy, growing organization for God's Kingdom.

The workbook nor the book *Reaching the Summit* has been written to be covered in a weekend retreat or other short-term setting. This is not a quick-fix for any organization. (That would be a phase four savior mentality, which this material firmly instructs against.) Rather this is to be perceived and used as a guide to a process for building healthy practices and tenets for prolonged health inside a growing organization.

Each module in this guide and each corresponding chapter(s) in *Reaching the Summit* should be covered thoroughly and completely before moving on to the next. Prayer is a large part of the process for leading and guiding your team and your organization through this process. Do not overlook the importance of meaningful time in prayer before, during, and after each module. The life and future of your organization depend on it.

If you have not considered or settled on a consultant/coach to assist you through this process, let me encourage you right now to consider it before moving any further. This could be one of the greatest and most beneficial steps in the entire process. There are many reasons given in Reaching the Summit for bringing on a consultant/coach from the outside. Two of the major reasons are: 1) the outside coach sees from a different, more objective perspective than anyone on your team. 2) A trained and experienced coach is experienced in developing the questions needed to assist your team in reaching for the summit.

For more information on selecting a consultant/coach or for possible available coaches for your specific organization please contact SonC.A.R.E. Ministries through our website: **soncare.net**

Take a deep breath, pray, and begin your journey in reaching your God-given summit.

The Five Phases of Decline

Early stages of decline in the church often go un-noticed. The longer a church lives in this mindset, the further into decline it will descend and the purpose or mission moves from reaching the lost for Christ, to

"We're here, we hope you come." to

"If they come they come, if not it is their fault." to

"Why aren't we growing, they won't come." to

"I just don't know what happened, we tried."

If you had to choose one of the above statements for your church, which one would best describe your church's heart-felt actions today? Circle the statement you choose.

The five phases of decline are listed throughout this work as:

Phase one – Loss of Vision

Phase two – Lack of Purpose

Phase three – Denial

Phase four – Grasping for Survival

Phase five - Relinquishment of Ministry

After reading Section One (which includes the first five chapters) of *Reaching the Summit,* based on your perspective, place a check mark beside the phase listed above that best describes the position of your church today.

Write a brief explanation of why you chose this particular phase as representative of your church's situation.

_____

_____

_____

_____

_____

Before moving on, review the chapter depicting the phase you chose. (If you are working in a group from your church, come to a consensus of which phase is most representative of your church). Find areas in the chapter that particularly stand out to you as characteristic of your church today. List those below.

_____

_____

_____

_____

_____

By what you've read in section one, what do you believe as a church you can work on to change the mindset and reverse the trends of decline in your church?

_____

_____

_____

_____

_____

Judges chapter 13 through 16 tell the story of Samson, a man set apart by God to be His servant leader. Samson was blessed by God above other men. He had incredible strength. With this blessing of strength Samson killed a lion with his bare hands. He killed 1,000 fighting men (soldiers) in one day using the jawbone of a donkey. God had given Samson strength greater than 1,000 men to be used by God against Israel's enemies.

Samson had a weakness. His weakness was women. And he let his weakness consume his strength. In his weakness Samson not only lost his strength. His enemies gouged out his eyes and made Samson a blind slave. He lived the rest of his days in shackles. But as his hair grew back Samson regained his strength. And in his final act of service to God and in one display of strength scripture tells us he killed more of God's enemies, the Philistines than he had killed in all his battles before.

Samson's comeback also took his life. Our comeback does not need to. However, I believe there is a great lesson here. Samson finally surrendered his all to the Lord. No matter what phase of decline we find ourselves in, when we come to a point of total surrender to God, this is when we will see the greatest victory. How close are you to coming to this point of total surrender?

_____

_____

What is hindering you from reaching that point today?

_____

_____

Before moving on to the identifying and planning stages for your church there is a season needed, a season of soul-searching prayer. This prayer time cannot to be taken lightly. This is where we draw the battle lines against Satan. This may be one of the most important times of prayer in the entire existence of your church. I have introduced this as a prayer season. Five minutes of prayer will not do. If you and your church leaders are serious about reversing declining trends in your church and furthering God's kingdom this must receive the upmost priority and importance. Perhaps your leadership team should pray about the length of your church's season of prayer. Should it be one week, two, one month, or perhaps forty days?

In your season of prayer you should include:

1. Praise and adoration to a God (the only true God) who has blessed you immensely and given you an opportunity to serve Him along with the other members of your church. Read Psalms 103 three times as follows. 1) Read the Psalm as it is written. 2) Read it a second time replacing the words you, yours and similar with your name (church name). 3) Read the Psalm as a prayer of praise to God for what He has done for your church.

Praise God for *whatever is true, whatever is honorable, whatever is just, whatever is pure, whatever is lovely, whatever is commendable—if there is any moral excellence and if there is any praise—dwell on these things.* (Phil 4:8)

God has richly blessed us and deserves our praise.

2. Confession – We live in the flesh therefore we have a sinful nature. Even as redeemed believers the Bible considers our best works as only dirty rags compared to God's righteousness.

For all have sinned and fall short of the glory of God. Romans 3:23 (HCSB) In all our churches, we have not lived up to the potential God has bestowed upon us. If your church is facing even the slightest impression of decline confession is due to God for our lack of fulfilling His purpose for the church. Until each one realizes we all have fallen short of God's desire, your church will not make the turn to reach its potential.

For this portion of your season of prayer it is important to identify some of the possible areas of ministry and Christian living where your church is not meeting God's desires and standards. To remember these in prayer list each one here:

_____

_____

_____

_____

_____

Include in your season of prayer confession to God for these shortcomings. Next ask God to reveal other areas of needed change or improvement.

3. Petition – an appeal or request to a higher authority or being.

During your season of prayer petition God for His undeniable presence and guidance throughout the process you are about to undertake. List your desired petitions below. (You'll want to review these through the process to celebrate the victories as God moves you through progression. Some of your petitions may need revising.)

_____

_____

_____

_____

_____

There are many options you can take to draw your team and church into this season of prayer. Your team should pray examine and contemplate various options that could involve your leadership team, specific groups (deacons, elders, Bible study classes, etc.) and the congregation.

For example your leadership team will likely have a closer and stronger feeling for the needs of this prayer season leading to reversing decline. Therefore, this team's prayer effort will be more concentrated and resolute. For your congregation you might want to provide opportunities for members to come together and pray. Providing congregants with a scripture (as Phil. 4:8) to read and pray through each week is a great way to involve your church throughout the week. Remember, you cannot pray too much.

Examples:

- Prayer calendar for the church and the Reaching the Summit (RTS) Process

- Printed daily devotion to handout each Sunday for the week (4-6 weeks)

- Special prayer time in each service for the RTS process

- Church-wide fast

- Prayer emphasis email, text, or robo call

- Prayer cottages – in home prayer meetings with special emphasis on RTS

- Prayer vigil – 12 or 24 hour prayer vigil with members each taking a time segment to pray

Chapter 6 - Filling Positions With the Right People

Reading through scripture we find sometimes odd and obscure group of people whom God chose to use to fill positions of leadership and carrying out his will. I have a copy of a satiric letter someone wrote about the twelve men Jesus called to follow Him as disciples. The letter states that eleven of these men showed no capacity for leadership and suggested Jesus should replace them for they were not capable of carrying out His work. In the eyes of this modern day leadership consultant group the only one of Jesus disciples who Jesus should keep was Judas Iscariot. As I said it is a satirical (humorous spoof) letter, but what sad truth can be found in it. Often times what the world looks at as quality leader skills and ability, falls very short of what is needed for true quality leadership.

What process does your church routinely use for filling positions in the ministries of the church?

_____

_____

In your own words explain capacity as described and illustrated in this chapter. (Discuss answers with your team)

_____

_____

What characteristic qualities are found in a person of capacity? (Team Discussion)

_____

_____

How can we as a church leadership team help to build capacity in people holding leadership positions?

_____

_____

To lead is to use influence and to show the way. To manage is to have power over or to restrain. Briefly describe a time when you were managed or managed someone else when it would've been more productive to lead.

_____

_____

_____

How is the recruiting process in your church different from the one described in chapter six?

_____

_____

Is your church more interested in finding people of capacity and passion or finding a warm body to fill an empty slot? Give a brief explanation.

_____

_____

List three steps your church or ministry can implement to move towards insuring you have the right people in positions of leadership.

_____

_____

_____

Questions to ask potential leaders before filling any position: The following questions are examples of questions to ask to help you determine the candidate's potential in areas of teamwork, personal motivation, followership, leadership, and communication.

Describe the work environment or **culture** in which you are most productive and happy.

What goals, including career goals, have you set for your life?

What actions and support, in your experience, make a team function successfully?

Have you been a member of a team that struggled or failed to accomplish its goal? If so, what assessment did you make of the reasons for the failure?

In your opinion, what are the three most important factors that make you an effective, valued coworker? Give me three examples from your past work experiences that demonstrate these factors.

Tell me about a time when you disagreed with the actions or decisions of your manager or supervisor. How did you approach the situation?

What are the characteristics exhibited by the best boss you have ever had - or wished that you have had?

Relate to me (us) an occasion when you needed to choose between two or three seemingly equally viable paths to accomplish a goal. How did you make your decision about the path to follow?

Describe a working environment and its communication style in which you experience the most success.

While some may feel this is a bit over the top for recruiting volunteer positions, the more you know about someone's beliefs, interactions, and abilities, the better positioned you will be to make a wise decision for filling a position.

A couple of traits to watch for:

Does the person speak in only first person using a lot of "I" and "me" in his/her answers or do they share the stage and pass the credit?

In her answers about failures, missed goals, and former co-workers and supervisors does she issue a lot of blame and degradation to others without accepting or shouldering part of the responsibility?

Chapter 7 - A Vigorous Face to Face Summit with Reality

After I arrived in Jerusalem and had been there three days, [12] I got up at night and [took] a few men with me. I didn't tell anyone what my God had laid on my heart to do for Jerusalem. The only animal I took was the one I was riding.

[13] I went out at night through the Valley Gate toward the Serpent's Well and the Dung Gate, and I inspected the walls of Jerusalem that had been broken down and its gates that had been destroyed by fire. [14] I went on to the Fountain Gate and the King's Pool, but farther down it became too narrow for my animal to go through. [15] So I went up at night by way of the valley and inspected the wall. Then heading back, I entered through the Valley Gate and returned.

[16] The officials did not know where I had gone or what I was doing, for I had not yet told the Jews, priests, nobles, officials, or the rest of those who would be doing the work. [17] So I said to them, "You see the trouble we are in. Jerusalem lies in ruins and its gates have been burned down. Come, let's rebuild Jerusalem's wall, so that we will no longer be a disgrace." [18] I told them how the gracious hand of my God had been on me, and what the king had said to me. Neh 2:11-18 (HCSB)

A vigorous face to face summit with reality requires an intense look at the situation from the outside in as well as he inside out.

What is a Face to Face Summit with Reality?

_____

_____

Why is it best to have an experienced consultant/coach from outside the church assist you with this Summit?

_____

_____

What will a seasoned coach from outside the organization bring to the discussion for your church?

_____

_____

List three things from this chapter that you believe are of utmost importance. Did the Holy Spirit enlighten you with any of the elements of this chapter? Explain:

_____

_____

_____

Where to look and what to look for

Behavior Patterns – What similarities can be found by reviewing past decisions of the church? How has the church acted, reacted, or voted on sensitive issues?

_____

_____

_____

Trends – What is the difference between trends and behavior patterns? As a team identify trends that may be contributing to decline in your church.

_____

_____

_____

How do *character traits* often differ from behavior patterns in a church? Identify character traits of your church and plan a three to five step process to improve the character of your church.

_____

_____

_____

_____

_____

Inclusion – Reading the scripture from Matthew 8:9-13, prayerfully consider how your church practices inclusion and allow the Holy Spirit to guide you to particular areas your church needs to improve on inclusion.

_____

_____

_____

_____

Can you list the *core values* of your church – the true core values being manifested through church members throughout the week? (Determining & writing core values)

_____

_____

_____

_____

A person's actions are the outward manifestations of his/her core values. The same is true with every church. Therefore, the actions of the church are outward demonstrations of actual core values. Are your church members truly active in evangelism and inviting new people to church? If so, then evangelism might be a true core value. If not…

How can your church know that you are identifying and attempting to meet the true needs of the community?

_____

_____

What are you willing to do to lead your church or particular ministry to identifying and meeting community needs for the sake of sharing the gospel?

_____

_____

_____

Develop a strategy for identifying and meeting needs in the community.

_____

_____

_____

_____

_____

It is important to use caution when identifying needs and developing the strategies. The goal of this **Vigorous Face to Face Summit with Reality** is not to complicate your ministry but to help you to move toward a simpler yet kingdom productive ministry. Another good resource to assist in this is the book "Simple Church" by Tom Rainer and Eric Geiger (Broadman & Holman)

Chapter 8 - Understanding the Necessity of the Situation

Nehemiah 1:1-11 (HCSB)

During the month of Chislev in the twentieth year, when I was in the fortress city of Susa, 2 Hanani, one of my brothers, arrived with men from Judah, and I questioned them about Jerusalem and the Jewish remnant that had returned from exile. 3 They said to me, "The survivors in the province, who returned from the exile, are in great trouble and disgrace. Jerusalem's wall has been broken down, and its gates have been burned down."

4 When I heard these words, I sat down and wept. I mourned for a number of days, fasting and praying before the God of heaven. 5 I said, LORD God of heaven, the great and awe-inspiring God who keeps His gracious covenant with those who love Him and keep His commands, 6 let Your eyes be open and Your ears be attentive to hear Your servant's prayer that I now pray to You day and night for Your servants, the Israelites. I confess the sins we have committed against You. Both I and my father's house have sinned.

7 We have acted corruptly toward You and have not kept the commands, statutes, and ordinances You gave Your servant Moses. 8 Please remember what You commanded Your servant Moses: "[If] you are unfaithful, I will scatter you among the peoples. 9 But if you return to Me and carefully observe My commands, even though your exiles were banished to the ends of the earth, I will gather them from there and bring them to the place where I chose to have My name dwell." 10 They are Your servants and Your people. You redeemed [them] by Your great power and strong hand.

11 Please, Lord, let Your ear be attentive to the prayer of Your servant and to that of Your servants who delight to revere Your name. Give Your servant success today, and have compassion on him in the presence of this man.

When Nehemiah heard of the plight and condition of Jerusalem what were his first actions as described in Nehemiah 1:1-11.

_____

_____

Moving the answers from the summit to perceptive aspect of ministry.

Once the open and true reality of the situation, the brutal facts, have been laid out, what is necessary for your church to move forward?

_____

_____

_____

_____

_____

What steps can you take as a church leader and as a church to insure you are getting an open an honest assessment of your ministry situation?

_____

_____

_____

_____

_____

Identifying with the necessity of the situation

In your own words describe the difference between identifying the situation and identifying <u>with</u> the situation.

_____

_____

_____

In Nehemiah chapter one, verse four Nehemiah writes, "*I sat down and wept. I mourned for a number of days, fasting and praying before the God of heaven.*" Nehemiah set everything aside. He fasted, went without eating, and he prayed – for days. Read Nehemiah's prayer beginning in verse 5.

Before moving beyond this point in the study, using Nehemiah's prayer as a prompt, enter into a time of prayer for your ministry and your church. Listen to the Holy Spirit. List below any thoughts the Holy Spirit brings to your mind during your prayer time.

_____

_____

_____

Taking personal responsibility

Are you willing to take the necessary steps? ____Yes ____ No

Are you willing to accept personal responsibility? ____Yes ____ No

To what degree are you willing to take personal responsibility? _____

_____

What are your reservations?

_____

_____

What is the greatest advantage of taking the necessary steps?

_____

_____

_____

What is the desired outcome if these steps are carried through?

_____

_____

_____

Begin working to develop a timeline for your church in seeing and understanding steps needed to identify with the necessity of the situation and to work in strategy planning to address the necessities.

_____

_____

_____

Chapter 9 - The One Best Thing

Exodus31:1-7 – Bezalel, **The LORD also spoke to Moses: ² "Look, I have appointed by name Bezalel son of Uri, son of Hur, of the tribe of Judah. ³ I have filled him with God's Spirit, with wisdom, understanding, and ability in every craft ⁴ to design artistic works in gold, silver, and bronze, ⁵ to cut gemstones for mounting, and to carve wood for work in every craft.**

⁶ I have also selected Oholiab son of Ahisamach, of the tribe of Dan, to be with him. I have placed wisdom within every skilled craftsman in order to make all that I have commanded you: ⁷ the tent of meeting, the ark of the testimony, the mercy seat that is on top of it, and all the [other] furnishings of the tent...

Why did God instruct Moses to have Bezalel, Oholiab, and Ahisamach to such a special work?

_____

Phil 4:15-20 (HCSB)

And you, Philippians, know that in the early days of the gospel, when I left Macedonia, no church shared with me in the matter of giving and receiving except you alone. ¹⁶ For even in Thessalonica you sent [gifts] for my need several times. ¹⁷ Not that I seek the gift, but I seek the fruit that is increasing to your account.

¹⁸ But I have received everything in full, and I have an abundance. I am fully supplied, having received from Epaphroditus what you provided—a fragrant offering, a welcome sacrifice, pleasing to God. ¹⁹ And my God will supply all your needs according to His riches in glory in Christ Jesus. ²⁰ Now to our God and Father be glory forever and ever. Amen.

In this passage Paul is exhorting the believers at Philippi? Was his exhortation because they gave to him? ___Yes ___No Explain:

_____

_____

Explanation of the One Best Thing

If all barriers were removed, what is the one thing you would be doing for God?

_____

_____

_____

What is keeping you from this one thing?

_____

_____

_____

How to begin to determine your "one best thing."

Define purpose and passion as described in this chapter.

_____

_____

_____

_____

To what degree are you as a church leader willing to commit to achieve the explicit intent of the church to fulfill the purpose of the church?

_____

_____

_____

Before moving on it is again time to pray. Pray asking God to assist you in seeing and understanding what His specific purpose for your church is and how to lead your church in discovering the uniqueness of fulfilling that purpose as a body of believers. Ask God to open your eyes, mind, and heart to receive from Him what you have as a church failed to see or believe in the past.

In your own words describe the meaning of the statement, "_Do not copy models, capture principles._"

_____

_____

_____

How has the extent of your intent directed your church over the past ten years?

_____

_____

_____

In thirty words or less describe the one best thing your church can and should focus on.

_____

_____

_____

Chapter 10 -Vision - the Compelling Image of an Achievable Future

Genesis 41:28-40 *"It is just as I told Pharaoh: God has shown Pharaoh what He is about to do. ²⁹ Seven years of great abundance are coming throughout the land of Egypt. ³⁰ After them, seven years of famine will take place, and all the abundance in the land of Egypt will be forgotten. The famine will devastate the land. ³¹ The abundance in the land will not be remembered because of the famine that follows it, for the famine will be very severe.*

³² Because the dream was given twice to Pharaoh, it means that the matter has been determined by God, and IIe will soon carry it out. ³³ "So now, let Pharaoh look for a discerning and wise man and set him over the land of Egypt.

³⁴ Let Pharaoh do this: Let him appoint overseers over the land and take one-fifth [of the harvest] of the land of Egypt during the seven years of abundance. ³⁵ Let them gather all the [excess] food during these good years that are coming, store the grain under Pharaoh's authority as food in the cities, and preserve [it] . ³⁶ The food will be a reserve for the land during the seven years of famine that will take place in the land of Egypt. Then the country will not be wiped out by the famine."

The proposal pleased Pharaoh and all his servants. ³⁸ Then Pharaoh said to his servants, "Can we find anyone like this, a man who has the spirit of God in him?" ³⁹ So Pharaoh said to Joseph, "Since God has made all this known to you, there is no one as intelligent and wise as you. ⁴⁰ You will be over my house, and all my people will obey your commands. Only with regard to the throne will I be greater than you."

In this passage the king of Egypt recognizes Joseph as a man who not only reads the vision of a dream, but as a man of capacity and one who is able to set the path and vision for the nation. Joseph has a compelling vision for an achievable future.

What is a vision – Using the information at the beginning of chapter ten (10) in your own words write a summary of what is a vision for the church.

_____

_____

_____

What is your perception of your church's vision in terms of spiritual transformation for the next year and beyond? What could be evidence of spiritual growth in the lives of the people in your church?

_____

_____

_____

What is your perception of your church's vision in terms of Ministry Expansion for the next year and beyond? Does the church as a whole encourage and provide opportunities for members to minister? If yes, identify at least one.

_____

_____

_____

How do your Small group Bible study classes and other ministries currently support missions? What can you do to promote active involvement in mission minded ministries to your church members through the various ministry avenues of your church? How will this support the vision of the church?

_____

_____

_____

_____

What is your perception of your church's vision in terms of numerical growth for the next year and beyond? Do you truly expect numerical growth through your Sunday School and other ministries?

_____

_____

_____

Identify some numerical goals for your church and small group Bible study classes and other ministries. *What will you do to promote the achievement of these goals? How will this assist in fulfilling the vision of the church?*

_____

_____

_____

Steps in preparing a vision (scripture suggestions) Some of the questions to be asked to begin the defining process of a vision are:

Where are we now?

_____

_____

_____

Where does God want us to be one year from now?

_____

_____

_____

Where does God want us to be five years from now?

_____

_____

_____

Are you willing and able to take on the task to fulfill God's vision for the church? List viable reasons for and hurdles you personally will face.

_____

_____

_____

_____

_____

What will be required for the church (body of believers) to accept the vision and carry it forward?

_____

_____

_____

_____

What steps will you implement for Recasting the Vision?

_____

_____

_____

_____

Chapter 11 - Moving The Locomotive

Joshua 3:2-*After three days the officers went through the camp ³ and commanded the people: "When you see the ark of the covenant of the LORD your God carried by the Levitical priests, you must break camp and follow it. ⁴ But keep a distance of about 1,000 yards between yourselves and the ark. Don't go near it, so that you can see the way to go, for you haven't traveled this way before."*

⁵ Joshua told the people, "Consecrate yourselves, because the LORD will do wonders among you tomorrow." ⁶ Then he said to the priests, "Take the ark of the covenant and go on ahead of the people." So they carried the ark of the covenant and went ahead of them … ⁸ Command the priests carrying the ark of the covenant: 'When you reach the edge of the waters, stand in the Jordan."

⁹ Then Joshua told the Israelites, "Come closer and listen to the words of the LORD your God." ¹⁰ He said, "You will know that the living God is among you and that He will certainly dispossess before you the Canaanites, Hittites, Hivites, Perizzites, Girgashites, Amorites, and Jebusites ¹¹ when the ark of the covenant of the Lord of all the earth goes ahead of you into the Jordan…

¹³ When the feet of the priests who carry the ark of the LORD, the Lord of all the earth, come to rest in the Jordan's waters, its waters will be cut off. The water flowing downstream will stand up [in] a mass." ¹⁴ When the people broke camp to cross the Jordan, the priests carried the ark of the covenant ahead of the people.

¹⁵ Now the Jordan overflows its banks throughout the harvest season. But as soon as the priests carrying the ark reached the Jordan, their feet touched the water at its edge ¹⁶ and the water flowing downstream stood still, rising up [in] a mass that extended as far as Adam, a city next to Zarethan. The water flowing downstream into the Sea of the Arabah (the Dead Sea) was completely cut off, and the people crossed opposite Jericho.

¹⁷ The priests carrying the ark of the LORD's covenant stood firmly on dry ground in the middle of the Jordan, while all Israel crossed on dry ground until the entire nation had finished crossing the Jordan.

To advance or move a group or organization ahead requires forward motion. All parts and all people must be moving and pulling in the same direction. When we do this under God's direction and not our own perceived path, we will accomplish great things in His power.

Using the information in the first two paragraphs of chapter 11 of *Reaching the Summit* what is needed to lead an organization to achieve success.

_____

_____

_____

_____

_____

In your own words write a comparison of Moving a Locomotive and the church.

_____

_____

_____

_____

According to the section on prayer (page 108) how should you lead your decision making team and church to pray? In the space provided below write the six listed in the text. What other areas are needed for your church to accept this decision?

_____

_____

_____

_____

_____

_____

_____

Why is community decision making important in the church?

_____

_____

Near the end of the section titled, *Moving the locomotive through different approaches,* three areas are listed for each ministry team leader. List these three and discuss the importance of each one in leading your church to healthy success.

_____

_____

_____

_____

What obstacles or sticking points need to be addressed before presenting this to ministry team leaders?

_____

_____

_____

_____

What great triumph do you envision after reading and studying this chapter on Moving the Locomotive?

_____

_____

_____

Chapter 12 - Organized Open Small Group Bible Studies

[41] So those who accepted his message were baptized, and that day about 3,000 people were added to them. [42] And they devoted themselves to the apostles' teaching, to fellowship, to the breaking of bread, and to prayers. [43] Then fear came over everyone, and many wonders and signs were being performed through the apostles. [44] Now all the believers were together and had everything in common. [45] So they sold their possessions and property and distributed the proceeds to all, as anyone had a need. [46] And every day they devoted themselves [to meeting] together in the temple complex, and broke bread from house to house. They ate their food with gladness and simplicity of heart, [47] praising God and having favor with all the people. And every day the Lord added to them those who were being saved. Acts 2:41-47 (HCSB)

In this biblical passage we see the early church and the functions of the church. Locate and list below the verses that speak of each of the five functions of the church.

Evangelism - _____   Ministry - _____

Discipleship - _____   Worship - _____

Fellowship - _____

If these are the five functions of the church and the Sunday School (small group Bible study) is the largest representative organization of the church should these not also be the five functions of Sunday School?

How are your open Bible study groups doing at carrying out the five functions of the church?

_____

Based on the opening paragraphs of chapter 12 in *Reaching the Summit*, list three qualities of an open small group Bible study or Sunday School class.

_____

_____

_____

Using the information in the text of this chapter <u>what does your church need</u> for building Passion for the following areas of a healthy, growing Open Bible study group strategy?

Passion for biblical equipping

_____

_____

Passion for community

_____

_____

Passion for Growing People

_____

_____

Passion for Prayer

_____

_____

Using the information in the text of this chapter how will your church build Strategic focus for each of the following areas of a healthy, growing Open Bible study group strategy?

Strategy for Equipping

_____

_____

Strategy for Growing People (disciples)

_____

_____

Strategy for Building Community

_____

_____

Strategy for Expansion

_____

_____

Strategy for engagement

_____

_____

Passion & Strategy for Celebrative Atmosphere

_____

_____

Build an atmosphere of passion, enthusiasm, and an intentional strategy for celebrating all the victories and accomplishments of ministries of the church. The celebration itself will encourage and motivate others to get on board and join in the ride – for the joyous ride of a lifetime.

Chapter 13 - Stalwart and Steadfast

Five times I received from the Jews 40 lashes minus one. Three times I was beaten with rods. Once I was stoned. Three times I was shipwrecked. I have spent a night and a day in the depths of the sea.

On frequent journeys, [I faced] dangers from rivers, dangers from robbers, dangers from my own people, dangers from the gentiles, dangers in the city, dangers in the open country, dangers on the sea, and dangers among false brothers; labor and hardship, many sleepless nights, hunger and thirst, often without food, cold, and lacking clothing. Not to mention other things, there is the daily pressure on me: my care for all the churches. 2 Corinthians 11:24-28 (HCSB)

Using the text from chapter 13, in your own words write an explanation of the two terms in the title of this chapter.

Stalwart

_____

_____

Steadfast

_____

_____

To have a stalwart belief is to be resolute in what you accept as true. In Daniel 1:8 we read: *"Daniel determined that he would not defile himself with the king's food or with the wine he drank. So he asked permission from the chief official not to defile himself."* Daniel had a stalwart belief. He was taking a huge risk and so was the steward responsible for Daniel's well being.

How do we build a stalwart belief in something?

_____

_____

To have a steadfast faith is to have an unwavering commitment to the assurance and trust in God for the unknown that lies ahead. The apostle Paul through many hardships and in prison maintained a steadfast faith.

Though the two terms are similar, write a brief explanation of how the two are separate yet complementary.

_____

_____

_____

Spiritual disciplines to build the two

What spiritual discipline elements are needed to bring your church to a stalwart belief and a steadfast faith?

_____

_____

You cannot force a stalwart belief or a steadfast faith. Each person must develop his own. What steps are you willing to undertake as leader(s) of the church to encourage and build a stalwart belief and steadfast faith in your church?

_____

_____

_____

_____

What signs will be evidence that you and your church are moving toward a stalwart belief and a steadfast faith?

_____

_____

Building and maintaining a stalwart belief and a steadfast faith is an on-going process for each believer and a church family. As you think through the process of building these into your congregation, what development practices can you implement to assist each member to continue growing in these two areas?

_____

_____

_____

_____

Choose a date now to revisit the works in this book for review and evaluation. Let me encourage you to evaluate progress every three months and come back to this book for review in six months and again one year from now. Stay on track and build in friendly accountability in moving your ministry forward for God's kingdom!

Spend time in prayer as a group of leaders for a stalwart belief and steadfast faith as you move forward with principles and practices to reverse declining trends and avoid future decline in your ministry.

www.ingramcontent.com/pod-product-compliance
Lightning Source LLC
Chambersburg PA
CBHW081235020426
42331CB00012B/3186